Training for Hyp

Muscle Growth

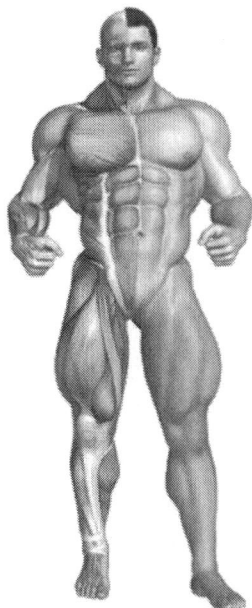

Health Learning Series

M. Usman

Mendon Cottage Books

JD-Biz Publishing

Disclaimer

The information is this book is provided for informational purposes only. It is not intended to be used and medical advice or a substitute for proper medical treatment by a qualified health care provider. The information is believed to be accurate as presented based on research by the author.

The contents have not been evaluated by the U.S. Food and Drug Administration or any other Government or Health Organization and the contents in this book are not to be used to treat cure or prevent disease.

The author or publisher is not responsible for the use or safety of any diet, procedure or treatment mentioned in this book. The author or publisher is not responsible for errors or omissions that may exist.

Warning

The Book is for informational purposes only and before taking on any diet, treatment or medical procedure, it is recommended to consult with your primary health care provider.

Our books are available at

1. Amazon.com
2. Barnes and Noble
3. Itunes
4. Kobo
5. Smashwords
6. Google Play Books

Table of Contents

Preface

There are oven a dozen approaches to how a person should workout, what supplements he/she should consume, or what time of day he should wake up in order to build muscle. Unfortunately, only a few of them make it to the top trusted list when there's time for a reality check. If the top charts are examined closely, any one could easily see that every approach that does make it to the top is something along the lines of "Lift Progressively Higher Weights and Eat Periodically".

Gym goers, as well as natural enthusiasts, have been too concerned with the tiny details of muscle building like insulin regulation, carbohydrates source, timing, muscle synthesis, and what not. All these signs and details are only vacillations that prevent them from admitting the truth behind their lack of commitment and technique. Thus, to save you from all this, this book will now explain the specific science behind muscle building, so that you'll know exactly how the body works and what must be done to accomplish muscle growth.

The book will tell you about "Muscle Hypertrophy"; read on and find out about this audibly heavy phrase!

Getting Started

Chapter # 1: Bigger & Better

What makes the muscles grow? Simply stated, when the human body is brought up against something heavy that causes a struggle in the muscles involved, it tends to develop stronger and bigger muscles the next time. This is so that lesser effort will be required the next time the same challenge comes up.

Hypertrophy is just a medical term that is synonymous for enlargement or growth of various areas in the body that may be muscles, organs, skins etc. But, a person only trains for the enlargement of his/her muscles and that is exactly the subject of this book. Call it hypertrophy, call it muscle growth; it is a process that is adaptive in nature and needs to be stimulated for proper growth. The demands are necessary for every person on the planet and no one can naturally induce hypertrophy without meeting them.

The muscles that make up the body are made up of motor neurons and muscle fibers, collectively known as Motor Units. The motor neuron is patched up with the brain through the spinal cord and the collection of all three entities makes up for the neuromuscular system, or more simply, the nervous system. In response to a load, the nervous system is responsible for sending signals to the muscles to contract so that the motor neurons can shorten or tighten the muscle fibers, creating tension. The number of motor units needed is directly proportional to the load. When muscle fibers are brought under tension, they start to lose energy in order to accomplish this, and if they are put under strain for a fairly long amount of time, they will completely lose their energy.

This means that the load alone is not necessary to create the required strain, but the frequency of strain is also necessary to stimulate growth. When enough strain is put on muscle fibers for a fairly long amount of time, messages are sent to the cells of the muscles to send back the details necessary to manufacture proteins from the amino acids present in the bloodstream. The amino acids integrate themselves into muscle fiber, thus increasing their cross sectional area, and thereby reducing the chances of a similar intensity workout the next time.

Muscle Hypertrophy increases in the hours following lifting, being at the highest point at time = 24 hours, and going back over the course of the next 48 hours. All in all, it takes 72 hours for the body to first induce hypertrophy and then bring it back to normal. It must be known that the body is constantly trying to balance between protein synthesis, known as anabolism, and protein breakdown, known as catabolism. For non-lifters, the effects almost cancel each other, which results in lower gain; a state known as homeostasis.

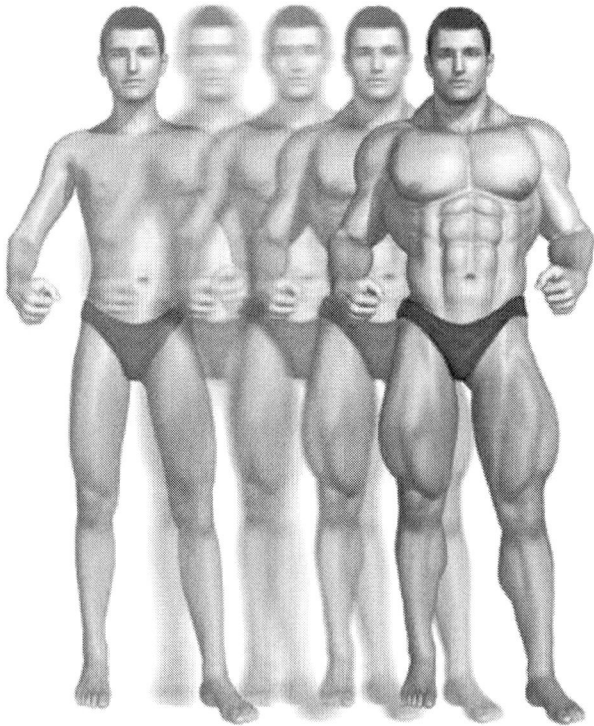

Growth can only be guaranteed if the muscle protein synthesis outranks the muscle protein breakdown. Thus, if you want to grow muscle, you must accomplish this task. The two greatest factors that increase muscle protein synthesis are lifting and eating protein/amino acids. What can increase it further is lifting while having amino acids in the blood stream. This effect is pretty much synergistic and is used extensively with the consumption of protein supplements. Still, tension has the largest effect on protein synthesis in the muscles; therefore, don't think that consuming loads of protein would just cause big muscles. If the stress is increased by *progressively* increasing lifting, the muscle will adapt further and get bigger in the process (filling the requirements needed for muscle hypertrophy). But, if the stress is repeated and not increased progressively, the muscle will go through a process known as accommodation and only become more efficient. Being more efficient, in turn means that the body will find ways to accomplish the task at the same size. This means that the muscle will remain the same diameter, not accomplish hypertrophy, whilst being able to carry out tasks at the equal intensity.

Chapter # 2: How Heavy?

It has already been said that the tension in the muscles depends on the load, which ultimately affects the number of Motor Units selected to carry out the lifting tasks. In the gym or during any activity that puts strain on the muscles, there are two factors that are very much responsible for production of muscles:

1.   Muscle Fiber Recruitment,

2.   Rate coding,

The first factor has already been covered in the previous chapter. What is rate coding? It is a well-established fact that messages sparked by the nervous system effectively control muscle relaxation and contraction. The strength of the contraction depends on the speed of the message.

Up to about 80 – 85% 1RM, a person can rely on his/her motor unit recruitment. Above this, no more recruitment takes place and only rate coding kicks in. The fiber will be made to contract harder, meaning that all the muscle fibers will be utilized. Below 80 – 85% 1RM, the greatest motor units only kick in when the muscle fatigue worsens at the end of a set. It would only make sense to recruit these largest units at first, as these have the highest chances of growth. Thus, the rep range is further limited to 5 - 8.

The minimum tension required for muscle hypertrophy has been defined, but that's not all it takes. A minimum frequency also needs to be set for hypertrophy to be activated properly. After much needed practical, as well as scientific, research it was found that 60 total reps/each body part, at a load of 15RM, are necessary for hypertrophy to take place. As the goal of this routine is to stimulate each and every muscle fiber, the programs involved should indulge all fibers right from the first rep.

If a person gets stronger in between 1RM & 15RM, he/she is bound to get bigger. Spending time in the lower as well as higher rep area will induce great benefits in the body. For instance, a focus on strength building between 1RM & 4RM will carry onto higher rep limits; however, a focus on higher reps will drastically improve waste removal and increase energy supply in the muscles.

Growth is stimulated by an adequate amount of work and load; muscle failure does not really depend or have an effect on it. The loads stated previously have been in between 5RM and 15RM which means that it is the max amount of mass a person can lift for 5 or 15 repetitions. A true 5RM does not reach failure, but instead a person succeeds in lifting the weights required to complete each set. Still, the question as to whether to reach failure or not is a much debated one, which will be settled in the next chapter.

Chapter # 3: Failure or Not

What causes failure when lifting? A variety of reasons are responsible for a person failing; at the heavy end (1-3RM) a person fails simply because he/she cannot work with the neural drive and not because the muscle fails. Towards the lighter end, 15RM, metabolic effects like energy depletion and waste products, cause the termination of a set. Thus, a point must be found in between these two lines to decrease failure time as much as possible. One other question that does stand up in a crowd is whether a person actually fails. According to research and studies, there isn't much of a difference between actually failing and giving up. Both equally affect the hormonal and neural status, which in most cases is negative. Still, many builders do go through the process of failing as part of their education, so as to recognize the difference between giving up and failing. Some programs even advocate failure and push the body to the limit, but this book advises against it. A person should stop as soon as he notices another set may be out of the question. If the load chosen is heavy enough, you will be able to stimulate the same amount of growth during the starting reps as another person does, at the last step.

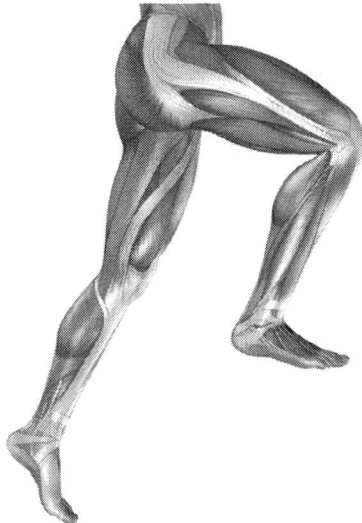

Chapter # 4: Getting Stronger

Muscle hypertrophy has been the subject of a lot of research and most of it has shown that after 72 hours muscle protein synthesis, remodeling, and all other processes return to normal. This provides us with a picture as to when muscles should be trained again. When training within appropriate parameters, once every 5 days or twice a week is an optimum time. Also, as your strength increases, the number of parts you are able to train each week decrease linearly.

Coming to the point, a person with really big muscles does not automatically make him extremely strong. In fact, strength comes from strong tissues, well-oiled joints, leverage, an efficient nervous system, etc. But, this also does not mean that a strong person won't have big muscles. Getting stronger does mean getting bigger, in a sense that the cross-sectional area of muscles increase, and with it a person's strength. Besides, having a really touched up nervous system, a big structure is also a prerequisite for getting significantly stronger. Hence, if you don't get stronger, you won't get bigger either; 1RM isn't the only measure of strength and if a person increases the strength from 6 -7 with 200 pounds, he/she is also bound to gain more strength.

The bottom line is that size comes from strength that is developed over the long term. If you won't work to get stronger, you won't get bigger either. Gutting down all those protein supplements won't magically build up the mass you want, but instead you'll become a loosely shaped, deformed lifter with no real power.

Techniques to Consider

Chapter # 1: Progression

Progression is a technique that is necessary if a person wants to induce full-scale hypertrophy. When a person starts lifting weights, his/her strength increases quickly and soon these increases take a linear path up, until a certain point. Think of yourself, if you kept on gaining strength linearly, a 5 pound increase in your squat would result in a 250 pounds worth squat in an year and in just 3 years you will be squatting over 1000 pounds! Therefore, when strength reaches a certain point, it becomes non-linear, but overall the trend should never face downwards. Some programs may focus on increasing sub-maximal loads with caution that would allow for more sustainable growth, but at the same time, one must bear in mind that muscle growth won't come as quick as one wants. Just as an example, you don't see your legs increasing in size every time you raise the bar.

There are various ways in which a person can progress:

i.   Single progression,

ii.   Double progression,

iii.   Triple progression,

iv.   Increasing only the reps,

v.   Increasing only the weight,

vi.   Auto-regulation

Of all the ways listed, the last one really stands out. It's not a new term and in fact, it's as old as they come. Auto-regulation exercise is a method where the next session's load is judged and adjusted, entirely using a statistical analysis of a person's current performance. Auto-regulation is very simple and can be followed simply by reading the cue your body gives to you each time you train. You may map out progression by planning in advance the increase in weights, as you are the best judge for yourself. But there's a drawback in the pre-determined technique, as you can't force progression if you're not ready. Just because you think you could do 5 pounds in the next session doesn't mean that you'll absolutely do it. They body will seem to play along with it at first, but will eventually fail. Furthermore, planned progression implicitly puts you in the loop that your performance would always be high. Let's face it; we all have our bad days, good days, and best days. Thus, it is best to judge in the current session, what you want to do in the next session.

Chapter # 2: Things to Ponder Over

Now comes Periodization, which is defined as the planning necessary to train in different manners or qualities; e.g. strength, endurance, and speed-strength, at different times, without losing the effects of the quality trained previously.

As the body has a finite capacity for recovery, a person cannot cover every sport, physical activity, and training method with equal focus, and that too, simultaneously. For hypertrophy, one does not need to worry about how much weights affect his/her sprint time or how to move with agility during a fight. Hypertrophy simply means getting bigger, and that can only be done by lifting, in simpler terms. The book recommends 6RM which is the range at which muscles are most exposed to fatigue and subsequent muscle stimuli. A person may also experiment above and below this range if he/she wants to in order to introduce the concept of Periodization in his/her regimen.

Focusing on a 1 – 5RM range will make you neutrally more efficient and stronger. As you get progressively stronger, your rep range will get bigger therefore, training in the 1 – 5RM range can positively benefit you. But, the 6RM range has been recommended because it will ensure enough strength without the need to go to lower rep ranges. Higher reps are good as they allow growth to stimulate and energy supply to improve, thus meaning that the connective tissues would be able to adapt to the max.

Another factor people tend to care about is the duration of the training session; the answer is simple. If a person closely monitors his /her workout, he/she would find that the length of a session truly depends on the number of sets and reps performed. If you have to warm up, cool down, perform lifting, and load over 600 pounds, a time between 40 and 90 minutes is just about right.

Chapter # 3: Exercise Selection

There are thousands of exercises from which you can choose. There is no way you can perform all of them, so being realistic, choose the ones that serve you best. It should be obvious, that as progression is the key, you should be more inclined towards exercises that allow progression. Typically, these exercises will revolve around barbell and dumbbells, but this does not mean that the exercises are limited to manmade equipment. Instead, you can start lifting progressively heavy rocks, but if you have easy access to a gym, that is preferred, because not only are progressively heavier rocks hard to find, but you are more likely to get yourself injured while lifting them. If you're sufficiently strong enough and no longer care about loading 400 pounds anymore, you may load it on a bench press and start lifting it. However, if you are looking for that one exercise that will target all your muscles, regardless of the equipment you use, you would be disappointed to find out that it doesn't exist.

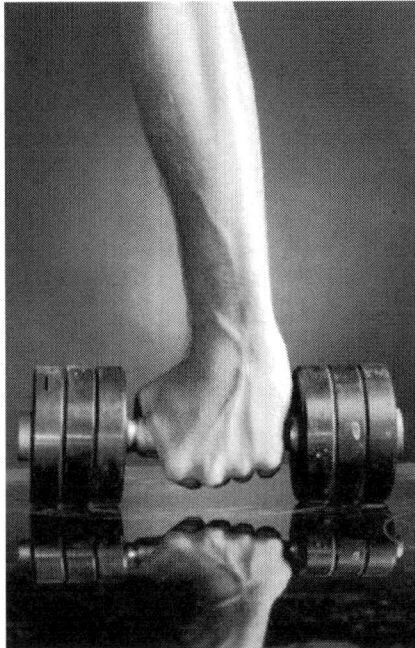

Applying common sense, you will soon find out that most of your exercises will be a mixture of compound movements with isolation. Some people think they can build enough mass just by using isolation exercises, but honestly speaking, this is not very true. To effectively train the whole body, one must resort to compound exercises.

Next, the functional vs. non-functional debate; the contractile components of the body make up for almost 80% of the muscle fiber, and the other 20% is sarcoplasm which is mostly liquid and required by every cell to function. Given that 80% of fiber is contractile version of protein, anyone whose muscles have grown must have hypertrophied this contractile tissue. So it would be the goal of this book to target this particular component through exercises.

If being able to run 7 – 10 miles, jumping through hoops while bench pressing is what you do, you might need to save children from a burning building, just to prove your point. In order to do all that, you must start training on all aspects of physical activity, which will distribute focus, leading to less mass, less strength, and less hypertrophy.

This book will follow a course that would train you to increase mass using the process of hypertrophy. The upcoming chapters are all about the details of the workouts.

Being Practical

Chapter # 1: Warm ups

Now that you're read all the theory on things and how they work it's time, you get your hands dirty by looking ahead to the practical tasks that await you.

Everyone's heard about warm-up exercises, and whether you like it or not, you must do them if you aim to achieve maximum strength. Most of these are boring drills like riding a bike, walking on a treadmill, or anything that will get you warmed up for the upcoming tasks. You'll be sorry if you skip these, as the body must be at the right temperature if you plan to ensure long-term muscle and joint functions. The following warm ups are recommended for anyone starting out on the hypertrophic training.

Upper Body Warm-up:

i.   15 reps of PNF diagonals,

ii.   Back and forth Shoulder circle, 30 seconds each

iii.   10 reps of Wall slides,

iv.   6 reps of explosive press-ups,

v.   6 reps of dumbbell snatch.

Lower Body Warm-up:

i.   15 reps of leg swings from side to side,

ii.   15 sets of leg swings from front to back,

iii.   10 reps of glute bridge,

iv.   6 reps of dumbbell swings

By now, you must be warmed up for the session. Now there would be only one exercise for each body part, while each exercise is worked at 6RM. Start with a barbell and increase the load, perform another rep, and increase the load once more. Perform yet another rep until you are ready to perform sets of six.

Now work your way up in sets of 6 to a sufficient weight that you can manage to complete for 6 good reps.

For instance:

i.   Bar x 6 reps,

ii.   135lbs x 1

iii.   185lbs x 1

iv.   And so on,

Now, rack the bar and rest as long as the body needs to recover. Attempt two more reps with a gap of 30 to 60 seconds. Rack the bar once more and breathe deeply for 30 seconds.

How many sets would it take to reach the 6RM barrier?

This is where auto-regulation comes in, as some days, it will be easier to reach the barrier, while some days difficult. You may feel like you are falling short at some point, but that's how nature works. This is how each warm up will be performed. In a race for the biggest gain, work your body to the limit so it can stimulate maximum growth. Once you surpass a certain amount of experience, strength gains would no longer be linear and you would only work to keep the trend from declining. Over the course of 4 weeks, you may experience all of the above, but the best thing to do would be to keep the graph rising.

It's been established that the strength gain should always have an upwards trend. With that said, the aim of the exercise should still be to break your personal best record in every session. Auto-regulation does mean working out at your own ease, but it should not act as an excuse to quit when you start to feel the intensity of a workout. In other words, if your body is bound to hit a PR in any session, you must make full effort that it does. You can't force progression, but you have to try to make it happen. If you are not ready to push your own record, the program won't be that effective for you.

Also, don't work the weights up in a tiny, micro-increment fashion. If you are strong enough, increase the weights by taking a five-pound step, but this does not mean to take huge leaps to get there, as that will only make matters worse. It is best to feel your way up. And the best advice is to not panic.

Chapter # 2: Exercise Performance

Between exercises and sets, it is also best to give your body a short break so that it can conjure up as much energy as possible. A hard stop of 2 minutes in between ramping sets and 30 seconds between clusters would be generous enough. If you think you can do anything that day, decrease the duration of the rest periods.

Builders like Doug Hepburn used to master weights to gain increasing amounts of strength. For instance, they tried their best to retain control, and move a weight powerfully at 6RM; you should do the same. When lowering the weight, don't give up on it, but take control of it, so that if a moment arises that you need to stop it and push it the other way, you could. (Also, don't artificially try to add length to the time!) An example of the concentric position would a bench press; when taking the bar away from your chest, imagine trying to push someone away, forcefully. It won't move as it should, but as long as you put energy in it, it's good. The feeling would be much more natural and different if you are not introduced to this way.

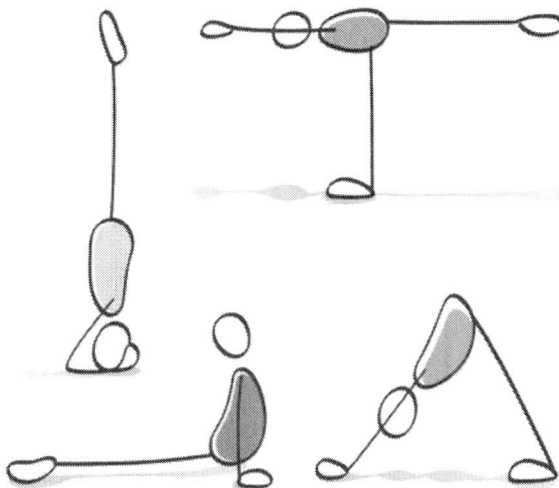

The prescriptions stated above can also be applied to calf exercises, and in fact, all of them.

Many readers will already be familiar with tons of exercises, enough to populate a dozen programs for weeks, but this book does make some suggestions of its own that can be helpful to people with no prior experience. But first, there is a word of advice; there may be some overlap in exercises, but this is a common happening in a body that never contracts a muscle under complete isolation. Whether you like it or not, some muscles will get worked along the main, target muscles.

A simple example is that of dead lifts and squats. In the program, it is advised to put rack pulls after squats for the reason that whichever way it is put, it will negatively affect a person's performance. A deadlift variation can be used straight from the floor, but only you can be the judge of how effective it will be. If a full deadlift was chosen, a leg press should be chosen after that.

The following table cunningly disguises the exercises in such a way that you won't leave any muscle unturned. Some people get really personal about upper body exercises, which leaves the lower body neglected and out of shape:

(One exercise per movement is advised per cycle)

Body part/ Movement	Exercise	
Horizontal pulling	i.	Pull-up,
	ii.	Chin-up,
	iii.	Rack chin,
	iv.	Pull down
Vertical pulling	i.	One-arm dumbbell row,
	ii.	Low pulley row,
	iii.	Barbell row,
	iv.	Hammer strength version

Horizontal pressing	i.	Incline bench press,
	ii.	Dumbbell bench press,
	iii.	Hammer strength version
Vertical pressing	i.	Standing dumbbell press,
	ii.	Standing barbell press,
	iii.	Hammer strength version
Triceps	i.	Dips,
	ii.	Reverse-grip bench,
	iii.	Close-grip bench,
	iv.	Overhead dumbbell,
	v.	Cable triceps extension
Biceps	i.	Dumbbell curl,
	ii.	Barbell curl,
	iii.	Hammer curl,
	iv.	Concentration curl,
	v.	Drag curl
Quad dominant	i.	Front squat,
	ii.	Back squat,
	iii.	Leg press,
Hip dominant	i.	Rack pull,
	ii.	Romanian deadlift,

	iii.	deadlift
Calf exercises	i.	Standing calf raises,
	ii.	Calf press,
	iii.	Seated calf raise
Abdominal exercises	i.	Barbell rollout,
	ii.	Cable crunch,
	iii.	Sprinter Crunch,
	iv.	Woodchops

Chapter # 3: Schedule

Now that you know about the exercises, you must also be told when to apply them. To help you with managing the exercises and workout routines, a plan has been put forward, given below:

For Week 1:

Monday:

- ✓ Horizontal pulling,

- ✓ Vertical pulling,

- ✓ Horizontal pressing,

- ✓ Vertical pressing,

- ✓ Triceps exercise.

Tuesday:

- • Rest

Wednesday:

- ✓ Quad dominant,

- ✓ Hip dominant,

- ✓ Calf exercise,

- ✓ Biceps exercise,

- ✓ Abs

Thursday:

- • Rest

Friday:

- ✓ Vertical pulling,

- ✓ Horizontal pulling,
- ✓ Horizontal pressing,
- ✓ Vertical pressing,
- ✓ Triceps exercise

Saturday & Sunday:

- Rest

For Week 2:

Monday:

- ✓ Quad dominant,
- ✓ Hip dominant,
- ✓ Calf exercise,
- ✓ Biceps exercise,
- ✓ Abs

Tuesday:

- Rest

Wednesday:

- ✓ Horizontal pulling,
- ✓ Vertical pulling,
- ✓ Horizontal pressing,
- ✓ Vertical pressing,
- ✓ Triceps exercise.

Thursday:

- Rest

Friday:

- ✓ Quad dominant,

- ✓ Hip dominant,

- ✓ Calf exercise,

- ✓ Biceps exercise,

- ✓ Abs

Saturday & Sunday:

- Rest

This is quite an easy program for anyone, as it involves hitting the gym only 3 times in a week. The approximate reps that will be executed would be somewhere around 35.

Chapter # 4: De-load Week

This is a specialized training week which applies to the schedule in the previous chapter, at the end of the 4th week. The aim of this particular week is to work in a more deviated line than the previous weeks. The aspect involved is that growth occurs when the intensity of the load is lighter which would require fatigue to really kick in. This in turn gives the joints and muscles of the body enough time to adjust back to normalcy.

The de-load week also follows the rule of one exercise per body part except this time the rep range is kept at 15 reps for every two reps. Once again, don't push yourself to failure, and just progressively increase the weight so that you hit comfortably, 2 sets of 15 reps each. This would only go on for a week; the details are:

For Week 1:

Monday:

- ✓ Horizontal pulling,
- ✓ Vertical pulling,
- ✓ Horizontal pressing,
- ✓ Vertical pressing,
- ✓ Triceps exercise.

Tuesday:

- Rest

Wednesday:

- ✓ Quad dominant,
- ✓ Hip dominant,
- ✓ Calf exercise,

- ✓ Biceps exercise,
- ✓ Abs

Thursday:

- • Rest

Friday:

- ✓ Vertical pulling,
- ✓ Horizontal pulling,
- ✓ Horizontal pressing,
- ✓ Vertical pressing,
- ✓ Triceps exercise

Saturday:

- ✓ Quad dominant,
- ✓ Hip dominant,
- ✓ Calf exercise,
- ✓ Biceps exercise,
- ✓ Abs

Sunday:

- • Rest

Chapter # 5: Supplements

1.   Protein Powder:

The name says it all. Protein is of prime importance to the muscles and to the body as well. But, for individuals who are struggling to reach muscle hypertrophy, protein plays a very important role. Intense training is responsible for a huge amount of stress on the body, which results in the muscle fibers tearing apart. They literally need to be repaired and remodeled and guess what particular compound is required for this? The answer is protein.

This book recommends that you consume at least 1.5 grams of powdered protein for each pound of body weight. Due to the fast pace of life, many individuals find it very hard to consume the right amount of proteins from foods, so the easy way is to gulp down protein supplements which are widely available in the market. These supplements come in various forms, stand-alone, lean mass, and meal replacements. Each variant serves a particular purpose but for hypertrophy, any supplement with a mixture of whey, egg proteins, and casein is recommended.

2.   Creatine Monohydrate:

This is one of the most studied and thereby proven ergogenic supplements ever produced by man. The majority of its users have reported gains in not only size, but also in strength after using it. Moreover, it has been proven safe and is known to contain a number of oxidant-inhibiting properties.

3.   Multi-vitamin:

Complete nutrition is one of the major pillars of the whole routine, designed to get your muscles into hypertrophy, but even with the most disciplined dietary practices, one always lacks the optimal level of minerals and vitamins. Thus, it becomes essential to fulfill the body's requirement by consuming vitamin supplements, also commonly available in the market.

4.   Fish oil:

A person also needs to have topped up levels of omega-3 fatty acids in order to completely be ready for a strenuous workout and it's after affects.

The complete details as to how the supplements need to be applied, is as follows:

60 minutes before workout (Have a solid meal):

- Carbs = 0.25g/lb. BW

- Proteins = 0.25g/lb. BW

- Fat doesn't really matter

30 minutes before workout (Have an energy drink):

- Carbs = 0.25g/lb. BW

- Proteins = 0.25g/lb. BW

60 minutes after workout:

- Carbs = 0.25g/lb. BW

- Proteins = 0.25g/lb. BW

- Fat doesn't really matter

Conclusion

And this completes an energetic journey to hypertrophy. It can be clearly seen how something so easy has been complicated to levels only master-builders could understand. The remarks of this book, even at signing off, would be to make a balanced diet a top priority of your life, as all the weights in the world could not life your body up to hypertrophy if the body does not have anything inside it. By following the diet, not only will you get bigger and stronger, but also you will feel good about yourself and life in general. In order to live a healthy life, you must bring physical activity to it, one way, or another. This book is for people who are looking to bring the "mega" factor into their bodies, so read it and best of luck applying it!

References

http://nl.123rf.com/photo_14317940_een-zeer-gespierde-man-afgebeeld-met-onderliggende-spier-structuur-aan-de-rechterkant--3d-render.html?term=muscle%20hypertrophy

http://nl.123rf.com/photo_15821697_illustratie-afbeelding-van-een-bodybuilder-het-verkrijgen-van-spiermassa-na-verloop-van-tijd--3d-ren.html?term=muscle%20hypertrophy

http://nl.123rf.com/photo_7877665_3d-rendering-van-de-mannelijke-beenspieren.html?term=muscle%20fibre

http://nl.123rf.com/photo_20653706_mannelijke-hand-houdt-metalen-barbell-op-donkere-grijze-achtergrond.html?term=muscle%20strength

http://nl.123rf.com/photo_24681070_halters-in-moderne-sportclub-weight-training-equipment.html?term=dumbbells

http://nl.123rf.com/photo_10358581_jongeren-beoefenen-van-yoga-voor-een-goede-gezondheid.html?term=gym%20routine

http://nl.123rf.com/photo_27251847_man-loopt-in-een-sportschool-op-een-loopband-concept-voor-het-uitoefenen-fitness-en-een-gezonde-leve.html?term=treadmill

Author Bio

Muhammad Usman is a distinguished medical graduate of Allama Iqbal medical college (AIMC). He is a professional writer who has been in the field for more than 4 years. During this time he has produced 10,000+ articles, blogs and eBooks on various niches related to diseases, health, fitness, nutrition and well-being. He is a regular contributor to several journals related to medicine and surgery. He is the editor of several journals and newspapers.

Check out some of the other JD-Biz Publishing books

Gardening Series on Amazon

Health Learning Series

THE MAGIC OF GOOSEBERRIES FOR HEALTH AND BEAUTY	THE MAGIC OF YOGURT FOR COOKING AND BEAUTY	THE MAGIC OF LEMONS USING LEMONS FOR HEALTH AND BEAUTY
THE MAGIC OF CHILLIES FOR COOKING AND HEALING	THE MAGIC OF ONIONS ONIONS IN CUISINE TO CURE AND TO HEAL	THE MAGIC OF RADISHES TO CURE AND TO HEAL
THE MAGIC OF CARROTS TO CURE AND TO HEAL	THE HEALTH BENEFITS OF OREGANO FOR COOKING AND HEALTH	THE Magic of MARIGOLDS Marigolds for Health And Beauty
THE HEALTH BENEFITS OF CINNAMON	THE MAGIC OF COCONUTS FOR COOKING & HEALTH	THE MAGIC OF CLOVES FOR HEALING AND COOKING
THE MAGIC OF ASAFETIDA FOR COOKING AND HEALING	THE MAGIC OF NEEM MARGOSA TO HEAL	THE MAGIC OF SALT TO HEAL AND FOR BEAUTY
THE MAGIC OF POMEGRANATES FOR HEALTH AND BEAUTY	THE MAGIC OF DRY FRUIT AND SPICES REMEDIES AND RECIPES	THE HEALTH BENEFITS OF TURMERIC CURCUMIN FOR COOKING AND HEALTH
THE MAGIC OF ALOE VERA	THE MAGIC OF VEGETABLES ANCIENT HEALING REMEDIES AND TIPS	THE HEALTH BENEFITS OF ROSEMARY FOR COOKING AND HEALTH
THE MAGIC OF PEPPER & PEPPERCORNS FOR COOKING & HEALING	THE MAGIC OF MILK, BUTTER AND CHEESE FOR COOKING & HEALING	THE MAGIC OF CARDAMOMS FOR COOKING AND HEALTH
THE HEALTH BENEFITS OF BLACK CUMIN FOR COOKING AND HEALTH	THE MAGIC OF BASIL-TULSI TO HEAL NATURALLY	THE MAGIC OF SPICES FOR HEALTH AND CUISINE
THE MAGIC OF ROSES FOR COOKING AND BEAUTY	The Miraculous Healing Powers of GINGER	The Miracle of HONEY

GRANDMA'S
NATURAL REMEDIES
AND ANCIENT HERBAL
BEAUTY RECIPES
Volume 1
HEALTH LEARNING SERIES
DUEEP J SINGH AND J DAVIDSON
GRANDMA'S
NATURAL REMEDIES
AND ANCIENT HERBAL
BEAUTY RECIPES
HEALTH LEARNING SERIES
DUEEP J SINGH AND J DAVIDSON
GRANDMA'S
NATURAL REMEDIES
AND ANCIENT RECIPES
GRANDMA'S CURE FOR OBESITY
GRANDMA'S CURE FOR THE COMMON COLD
Volume 3
HEALTH LEARNING SERIES
DUEEP J SINGH AND J DAVIDSON
GRANDMA'S
NATURAL REMEDIES AND
ANCIENT HERBAL RECIPES
Volume 4
HEALTH LEARNING SERIES
DUEEP J SINGH AND J DAVIDSON
GRANDMA'S
HERBAL LORE
ANCIENT HERBAL RECIPES AND REMEDIES
Volume 5
HEALTH LEARNING SERIES
DUEEP J SINGH AND J DAVIDSON
GRANDMA'S
ANCIENT
BEAUTY REMEDIES
FROM HER KITCHEN
Volume 6
HEALTH LEARNING SERIES
DUEEP J SINGH AND J DAVIDSON
GRANDMA'S
EASY TO USE TIPS
IN THE KITCHEN AND OUTDOORS
Volume 7
HEALTH LEARNING SERIES
DUEEP J SINGH AND J DAVIDSON
GRANDMA'S
HOUSEHOLD HINTS AND RECIPES
USING TIME TESTED
ECONOMICAL TIPS IN YOUR HOME
75 Tips
Remove Stains
Peel Tomatoes
Perfect Pies
HEALTH LEARNING SERIES
DUEEP J SINGH AND J DAVIDSON
GRANDMA'S
NATURAL REMEDIES
AND ANCIENT RECIPES
ALL 5 BOOKS IN 1
HEALTH LEARNING SERIES
DUEEP J SINGH AND J DAVIDSON

Country Life Books

A BEGINNER'S GUIDE TO RAISING SHEEP
DON'T BE DUMB ABOUT RAISING SHEEP..... BECAUSE THEY AREN'T
FARMING IN YOUR BACKYARD
JD-Biz Publishing
Darla Noble and John Davidson

A BEGINNER'S GUIDE TO RAISING DUCKS
KEEPING DUCKS IN YOUR BACKYARD
FARMING IN YOUR BACKYARD
PREPPING AND SURVIVAL BOOKS
JD-Biz Publishing
Dueep J Singh and John Davidson

A BEGINNER'S GUIDE TO RAISING TURKEYS
KEEPING TURKEYS IN YOUR BACKYARD FOR PLEASURE AND PROFIT
FARMING IN YOUR BACKYARD
PREPPING AND SURVIVAL BOOKS
JD-Biz Publishing
Dueep J Singh and John Davidson

FAMILY FARMING SAFETY
KEEPING KIDS SAFE ON THE FARM
COUNTRY LIFE BOOKS
JD-Biz Publishing
Darla Noble

CHICKENS ARE LIVESTOCK, TOO
A BEGINNER'S GUIDE TO RAISING CHICKENS
COUNTRY LIFE BOOKS
JD-Biz Publishing
Darla Noble

Turns Out you Can Grow Money
The Basics of Value-added Agriculture
COUNTRY LIFE BOOKS
JD-Biz Publishing
Darla Noble

Pretty & Practical
The Many Uses of Plants & Flowers
COUNTRY LIFE BOOKS
JD-Biz Publishing
Darla Noble

Ways to Sell What You Grow
Making Money with Your Farm
Selling Agricultural Products
COUNTRY LIFE BOOKS
JD-Biz Publishing
Darla Noble

Managing and Marketing SHEEP
TOOLS AND TECHNIQUES FOR EVERY SHEPHERD
COUNTRY LIFE BOOKS
JD-Biz Publishing
Darla Noble

Successful Shepherding
Management + Preparation = Healthy Sheep
COUNTRY LIFE BOOKS
JD-Biz Publishing
Darla Noble

Living Off the Land
A BEGINNER'S GUIDE TO BEING SELF-SUFFICIENT
COUNTRY LIFE BOOKS
JD-Biz Publishing
Darla Noble

Welcome to My Farm
Agri-tourism at its Best
17 Ways to Make Money From Your Farm
COUNTRY LIFE BOOKS
JD-Biz Publishing
Darla Noble

The Gardeners Pantry
Storing Away Food You Grow for the Winter
COUNTRY LIFE BOOKS
JD-Biz Publishing
Darla Noble

A BEGINNER'S GUIDE TO TRAPPING
TRAPPING TIPS AND TECHNIQUES
PREPPING AND SURVIVAL BOOK SERIES
JD-Biz Publishing
Shannon Rizzotto and John Davidson

OUTDOOR COOKING MEAT AND POULTRY
Grilling, Roasting and Braising Tips and Techniques
OUTDOOR LIVING SERIES
Dueep J Singh

PLANTS FOR SALE!
OWNING & OPERATING A GREENHOUSE FOR PROFIT
COUNTRY LIFE BOOKS
JD-Biz Publishing
Darla Noble

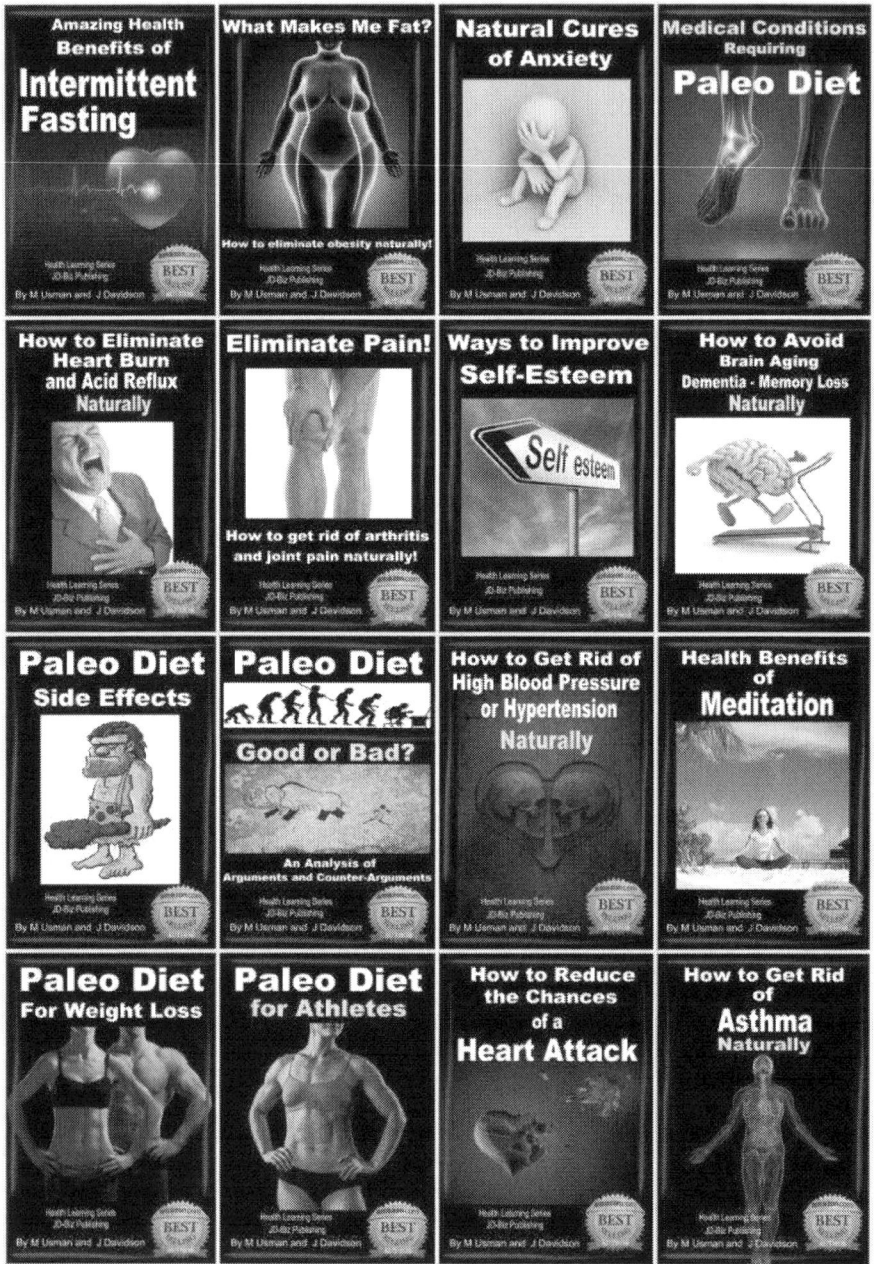

Amazing Animal Book Series

Chinchillas | Beavers | Snakes | Dolphins | Wolves | Walruses

Polar Bears | Turtles | Bees | Frogs | Horses | Monkeys

Dinosaurs | Sharks | Whales | Spiders | Big Cats | Big Mammals of Yellowstone

Animals of Australia | Sasquatch - Yeti Abominable Snowman Bigfoot | Giant Panda Bears | Kittens | Komodo Dragons | Lady Bugs

Animals of North America | Meerkats | Birds of North America | Penguins | Hamsters | Elephants

Learn To Draw Series

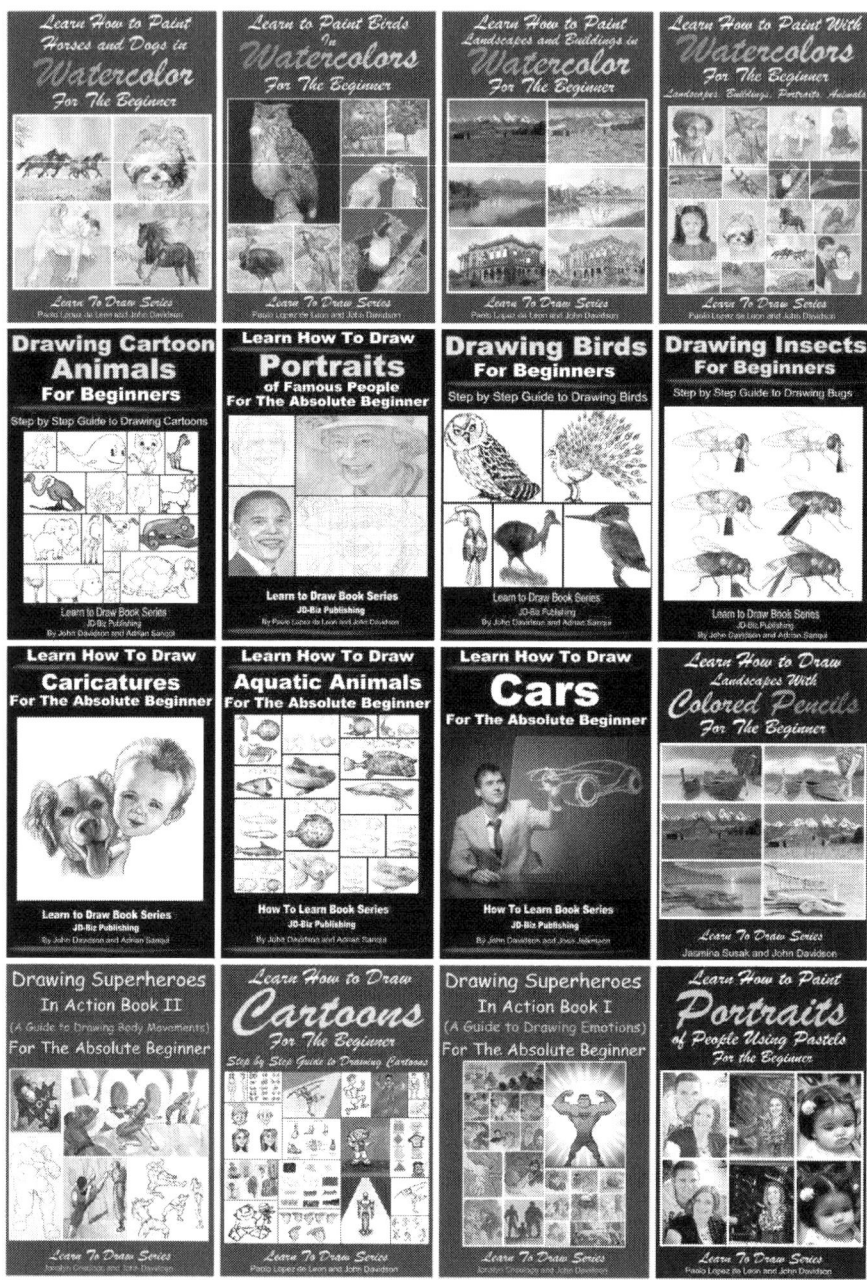

How to Build and Plan Books

Entrepreneur Book Series

Our books are available at

1. Amazon.com

2. Barnes and Noble

3. Itunes

4. Kobo

5. Smashwords

6. Google Play Books

Publisher

JD-Biz Corp

P O Box 374

Mendon, Utah 84325

http://www.jd-biz.com/

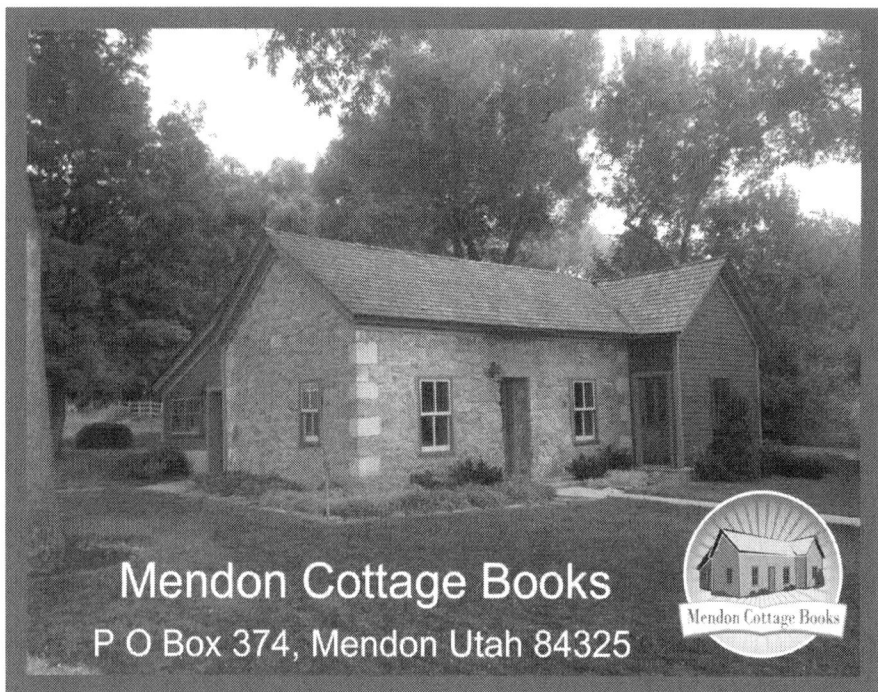

Mendon Cottage Books

P O Box 374, Mendon Utah 84325

6918597R00028

Printed in Germany
by Amazon Distribution
GmbH, Leipzig